Date Due			

AGAINST THE ELEMENTS

AIR

JANE WALKER

COPPER BEECH BOOKS • BROOKFIELD, CONNECTICUT

© Aladdin Books Ltd 1998

Designed and produced by
Aladdin Books Ltd
28 Percy Street
London W1P 0LD

*First published in the United States
in 1998 by*
Copper Beech Books,
an imprint of
The Millbrook Press
2 Old New Milford Road
Brookfield, Connecticut 06804

Printed in Belgium
All rights reserved
5 4 3 2 1

Editor
Simon Beecroft

Design
David West Children's Book Design

Designer
Robert Perry

Picture Research
Brooks Krikler Research

*Certain illustrations have been used in
previous Aladdin books.*

C.I.P. data is available at the
Library of Congress

ISBN 0-7613-0855-5

CONTENTS

Much of the air above our cities and towns is filled with a dangerous mixture of polluting gases (*above*).

Introduction

"We are tampering with the weather-making components of our atmosphere without knowing the outcome." *U.S. meteorologist, 1998*

We cannot see air. We cannot smell or taste air, and yet we are surrounded by it. Air covers the land and sea, and forms the atmosphere high above us. Without air, there would be no life on Earth because living things need the oxygen in air to stay alive.

Although air is invisible, we feel its effects when it pushes against us as wind. Wind can be a gentle breeze or a violent gusting wind, producing extreme weather conditions such as hurricanes and tornadoes. Experts are constantly working on ways to improve warning and information systems of severe weather, as well as defenses against the effects of strong winds when they do happen.

The layers of air that surround our Earth make up the atmosphere (*see* page 5). The atmosphere protects us from the sun's harmful rays, as well as trapping enough of the sun's heat to make the earth warm enough for us to live on.

Although the atmosphere is our life-support system, we are constantly filling it with harmful gases. The burning of fossil fuels such as coal and oil, and the destruction of rain forests, release harmful gases such as carbon dioxide into the atmosphere. The buildup of these harmful gases can change the entire climate of the globe. We are now faced with the challenge of protecting our planet's atmosphere for the next century.

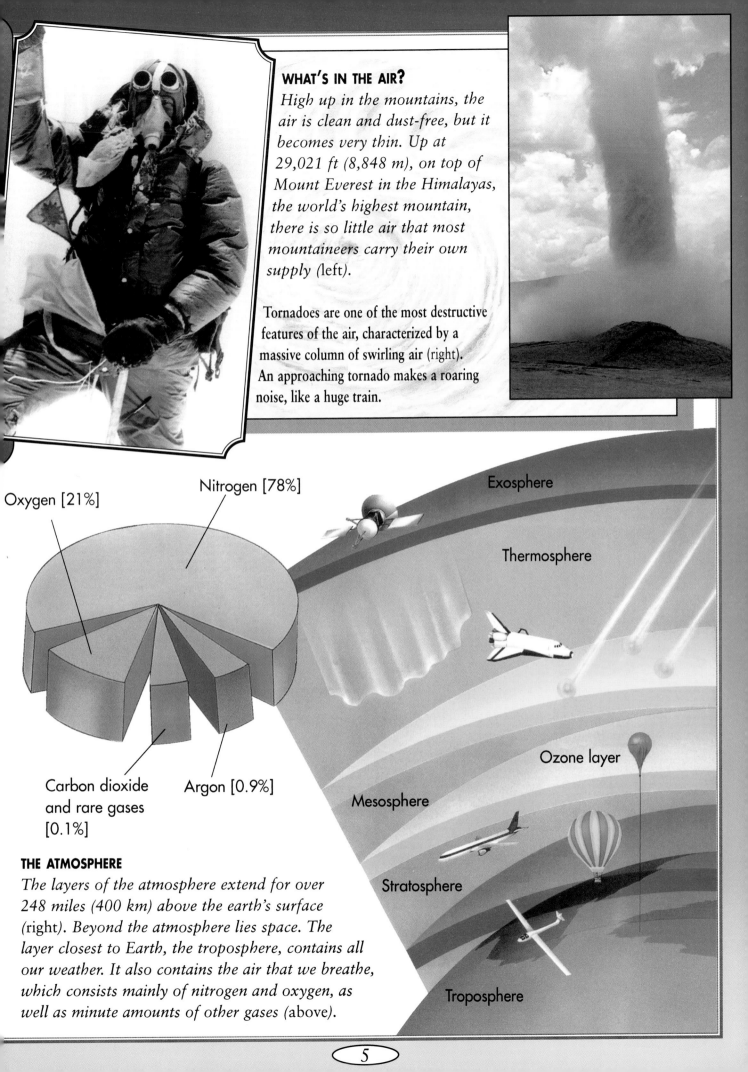

WHAT'S IN THE AIR?

High up in the mountains, the air is clean and dust-free, but it becomes very thin. Up at 29,021 ft (8,848 m), on top of Mount Everest in the Himalayas, the world's highest mountain, there is so little air that most mountaineers carry their own supply (left).

Tornadoes are one of the most destructive features of the air, characterized by a massive column of swirling air (right). An approaching tornado makes a roaring noise, like a huge train.

Oxygen [21%]

Nitrogen [78%]

Carbon dioxide and rare gases [0.1%]

Argon [0.9%]

Exosphere

Thermosphere

Ozone layer

Mesosphere

Stratosphere

Troposphere

THE ATMOSPHERE

The layers of the atmosphere extend for over 248 miles (400 km) above the earth's surface (right). Beyond the atmosphere lies space. The layer closest to Earth, the troposphere, contains all our weather. It also contains the air that we breathe, which consists mainly of nitrogen and oxygen, as well as minute amounts of other gases (above).

EL NIÑO

El Niño is triggered by a change in direction of the winds above the Pacific (right). As a result of the 1997 El Niño, almost no rain fell during Indonesia's rainy season, causing forest fires to burn out of control. In California, heavy storms brought huge waves crashing over the seafront. Local people protected their homes with sandbags (above).

Easterly winds Surface current Warm water Westerly winds Currents change direction

Normal year

Cool undercurrent

El Niño year

Warm water pushes toward coast

MONSOON SEASON

Between April and October, warm, moist monsoon winds bring torrential rains to southern Asia. The heavy rains are vital for a good harvest. The unwelcome effect of the monsoon is flooding which occurs when the region's rivers, such as Vietnam's Red River (left), burst their banks.

High winds

"Bill, your roof just blew right by my house ... Bill, your pump house just whipped by, too." Neighbors during storm, United States, 1985

High winds are caused by sudden and rapid movements of air across the earth's surface. They are caused by the uneven heating of the atmosphere by the sun: as air in one place is warmed, it rises, and cooler air flows in to replace it.

Today, organizations like the U.S. National Severe Storms Forecast Center (*right*) study weather information collected from satellites in space, weather balloons, radar, and weather stations on land and at sea. By building up a highly accurate picture of weather conditions, forecasters can use this knowledge to broadcast warnings of high winds and storm conditions. They use a special scale called the Beaufort Scale to describe wind speed. It ranges from 0 (calm) to 12 (hurricane). Hurricane-force winds blow at speeds of more than 74 miles an hour (118 kilometers per hour).

A particular change in wind direction causes an important weather phenomenon known as El Niño (*see* page 6). It occurs every three to eight years, when the southern Pacific Ocean off the coast of South America warms up, heating the usually cold waters off the coasts of Peru and Ecuador. The El Niño current influences weather patterns across the world, causing fire and drought in some places, and torrential rains and flooding in others.

THE GREAT STORM

Many people in southern England will never forget the night of October 15-16, 1987 (left). During this storm, hurricane-force winds killed 19 people, caused millions of dollars of damage to property, and blew down more than 15 million trees in one night. Chimneys toppled over, roofs were ripped off, walls were smashed into pieces, and roads and railroad tracks were blocked by fallen trees and telegraph poles.

This hurricane has been photographed from space. The calm cloudless area at the center is called the eye. Storm winds circle around it.

Hurricanes

"The most destructive storm — and the most expensive natural disaster — in U.S. history." Witness, Hurricane Andrew, 1992

Hurricanes are tropical storms that form over the warm waters of the North Atlantic and the North Pacific oceans. They are characterized by rotating winds that can reach speeds over 74 miles per hour (118 kilometers per hour), bringing heavy rain. Hurricanes tend to occur in a season that lasts from June to November. The first hurricane of each season is given a name beginning with the letter A (e.g. Hurricane Allen), the next one with B (e.g. Hurricane Betsy), and so on.

In the early morning of August 24, 1992, under cover of darkness, Hurricane Andrew struck the state of Florida. Winds tore through an area of more than 230 square miles (600 square kilometers). Within a few hours, the hurricane had demolished more than 80,000 homes, and severely damaged another 55,000, leaving more than 160,000 local residents with no roof over their head. In the local marina, yachts were snatched up and tossed around like toy boats — one was blown inland through the mangroves (*left*).

Hurricane damage can take a long time to repair. Roads have to be cleared of fallen debris so that relief workers can bring in emergency food and water supplies to the affected area. Electricity and telephone lines must be repaired so that contact with the outside world is resumed.

WHAT'S IN A HURRICANE?

A hurricane is a powerful swirling storm (right). It can measure about 300 miles (500 km) across. The storm clouds that surround the central, calm eye of the hurricane are known as wall clouds. The strongest winds and heaviest rains are found within these clouds.

Air swirls outward at the top

Eye

Spinning clouds

Bands of rain-filled wall clouds

Cold air is drawn in at the bottom

Columns of wind soar upward around the eye

DESTRUCTION AND DAMAGE

In Florida's Fairchild Tropical Garden, home to an important collection of palms and cycads, 70 percent of the plants were destroyed by Hurricane Andrew. After wreaking destruction in Florida (right), Andrew moved on to Louisiana. Here, it polluted vital fishing waters with debris and flattened the sugarcane crop.

HURRICANE INIKI

In September 1992, Hurricane Iniki created havoc and turmoil in the lives of the people of Kauai, Hawaii, in the Pacific Ocean. Many houses and other buildings were destroyed (left). In places likely to be affected by hurricanes, seawalls are built as a defense against storm surges (huge waves caused by hurricanes). Special shelters, raised off the ground and with strongly fortified walls, can also provide protection.

9

FLOOD ALERT

Much of Bangladesh's coastline is vulnerable to flooding during storms (above). One of the worst-affected areas is the densely populated area around the mouth of the Ganges River. Here, many people live and farm on mudflats formed by silt washed down by the river. Their makeshift homes are easily washed away by the floods.

AFTERMATH

After the 1991 cyclone, many Bangladeshis had no food and only contaminated, salty water to drink. Powerful storm surges had washed away most of the rice crop. Much-needed supplies of food and medicines were distributed (above) in an effort to prevent even more deaths — from starvation, dehydration, and disease.

The storm surges that accompanied the 1991 cyclone caused widespread flooding (*above*).

Cyclones and typhoons

"I heard the sound of an airplane, and saw a red fireball, as well as black clouds." *Eyewitness, cyclone in India, 1998*

Cyclone is the name of a storm with high, spiraling winds, such as a hurricane. Tropical storms in the Indian Ocean and to the north of Australia are called cyclones, while such storms in the western Pacific are called typhoons. (Shown *right*, the U.S. aircraft carrier *Hornet* was struck by a typhoon off Japan in 1945.)

Countries such as India and Bangladesh are regularly devastated by severe cyclones. The authorities have developed strategies for coping. Radar systems are used to give advance warning of approaching cyclones, so that people can be moved away to safety. In Bangladesh, evacuees are housed in cyclone shelters and concrete buildings on high ground. Seawalls and coastal vegetation such as mangrove swamps also provide some protection against storm surges.

In June 1998, a fierce cyclone hit India's western coast, its winds reaching 65 miles per hour (100 kilometers per hour). Hundreds of people were drowned by a 12-foot (4-meter) high wave that hit coastal villages. The cyclone changed direction suddenly before hitting land, which left people unprepared, and caused more deaths. The military and local rescue crews worked to remove the injured from collapsed buildings and take them to local hospitals.

The aftereffects of a cyclone or typhoon can also be serious. Water supplies are usually affected, and hospitals may be damaged. It is crucial that medical teams move in quickly to avert the possibility of widespread disease.

OPERATION REPAIR

A severe cyclone in Bangladesh in 1991 devastated homes (above) and left 10 million people homeless. An international aid effort was launched, and U.S. marines were drafted in to help build temporary shelters and deliver supplies, helping survivors to rebuild their battered homes (right).

Tornadoes and waterspouts

"I looked up and saw the stars. The whole roof was gone." *Homeowner, Florida, 1998*

Tornadoes are very powerful, swirling winds that occur during violent thunderstorms. The winds produced during a tornado are the most violent on Earth. A tornado is formed by air that rotates at high speed to form a narrow funnel that sucks up anything in its path. Central North America experiences more tornadoes than anywhere else on Earth (*far right*, a tornado which hit Texas, in May 1997).

With winds at its center reaching speeds of 200 miles per hour (320 kilometers per hour) or more, the tornado can destroy almost anything in its path. Trees are uprooted, buildings are smashed, and cars and other heavy objects are carried over long distances (*left*). A very destructive tornado can travel many hundreds of miles and may last for several hours.

In February 1998, a string of tornadoes battered the state of Florida, killing at least 30 people. Many of the casualties lived in mobile homes, which were picked up and tossed about by the high winds.

Japanese scientist Tetsuya Fujita makes miniature tornadoes (*above*). He creates them using dry ice so he can study the formation and behavior of these violent windstorms.

Descending air

Movement of tornado

Wall cloud

Funnel cloud

Dust envelope

HOW A TORNADO FORMS
Tornadoes usually occur on hot, humid spring days (right). As a thundercloud becomes dark and dense, the air at its base begins to rotate. This mass of twisting air forms a funnel cloud that extends slowly downward. As it touches the ground, dirt and objects begin to fly around, and an envelope of dust surrounds the tornado.

TORNADO OVER WATER

A tornado that forms over a lake or the sea is called a waterspout (above). It is a spinning column of air and mist that extends downward from a dark cloud, sucking up huge amounts of water. Waterspouts do not blow with as much force as tornadoes, and they usually last only about 15 minutes. They occur mainly in tropical parts of the world.

TWISTER

Tornadoes are also known as twisters. The movie Twister *(1996) follows scientists trying to track down and study tornadoes — and sometimes getting too close (above). American scientists engaged in the battle against tornadoes use a portable observatory called TOTO, named after Dorothy's dog in the book,* The Wizard of Oz.

A sandstorm blows through the city of
Khartoum, in the Sudan (*above*).

Shortage of trees
causes soil erosion

Over-grazing
by livestock

SPREADING DESERT

*Desertification, where
fertile land turns into
desert, is common in areas
with low rainfall and around
existing deserts, such as the Sahara.
However, various human activities are
causing desertification to increase (*right*).*

Wind blows
away topsoil

Over-farmed
soil

Trees are cut
down for fuel

LIMITING THE DAMAGE

*Thirty years ago, Nouakchott, the capital city of
Mauritania, in Africa, experienced about five days of
dust storms each year. Now, it has at least 80 days of
dust storms in a year. Barriers of trees and bushes
are planted to stop the advancing desert (*left*).*

Dust storms

"The dust was so thick that daytime was like night."
Eyewitness, dust storm in Mali, Africa, 1997

A dust devil (*above*) is a whirling column of air that carries sand and dust high into the air.

In a dust storm, strong, erratic winds carry fine particles of clay, silt, or other earthy materials over distances of hundreds of miles. Dust particles can be carried to heights of more than 1,000 feet (300 meters) by winds of about 25 miles per hour (40 kilometers per hour).

Dust storms occur in places where the ground has little or no protective vegetation because of low rainfall, overgrazing, or poor farming methods. They often occur in areas where drought is common (*below*), such as in parts of northern Africa.

In the 1930s, the Midwest was hit by severe dust storms, creating an area known as the Dust Bowl. These storms carried away millions of tons of soil and ruined harvests for many years, causing great hardship for farmers. Several factors contributed to the storms. In turning the area's natural grassland into wheatland, the farmers did not protect the soil from the wind, and the top layers of soil were carried away. Remaining areas of grassland were then ruined by the over-grazing of animals, and the situation was made worse by drought.

AMERICA'S DUST BOWL
During the great Dust Bowl era in North America, many farmers lost their crops and farm machinery, and faced bankruptcy. Food shortages became commonplace, and whole farming communities suffered serious hardship. Many poor farming families traveled west to try to rebuild their shattered lives (left). Conservation measures, such as planting trees to break the force of the winds, eventually slowed down the erosion and protected the soil.

VALLEY OF DEATH

The Brazilian town of Cubatão (left) is one of the most polluted places on Earth. Industrial plants, ranging from fertilizer factories to petroleum refineries, pump out thousands of tons of polluting gases. At times, the level of contamination is twice as high as that considered safe for humans, giving Cubatão a nickname of the "Valley of Death." Visitors to the town have reported experiencing a dull nagging ache in the chest within one hour after arriving in the town. The polluted air does not just affect the town's inhabitants. Crops, such as the banana plant (right), and livestock are also affected by the very high levels of pollutants in the air.

The greenhouse effect

"Our children are often ill, and sometimes can barely breathe."
Mother living in the "Valley of Death," Cubatão, Brazil

For millions of years, the so-called "greenhouse effect" has kept the earth at the right temperature to maintain life. A number of gases present in the atmosphere, known as greenhouse gases, trap the heat from sunlight and prevent some of it from escaping back into space. Now, scientists believe that the volume of greenhouse gases in the atmosphere has steadily increased, and too much heat has been trapped. They are concerned that these gases may be causing the world to heat up. This effect is known as "global warming."

The main greenhouse gas is carbon dioxide. Huge amounts of this gas are released into the air by human-made pollution, such as when forest areas are burned down (*below*), to clear land for farming and mining. As we burn fossil fuels such as coal and gas, we also increase the amount of carbon dioxide gas in our atmosphere.

The remaining greenhouse gases are methane (from animal waste, swamps, and oil and gas rigs), nitrous oxide (from car exhaust fumes), chlorofluorocarbons (from some aerosols, refrigerators, and foam products), and ground-level ozone (from the action of sunlight on exhaust fumes — see page 20).

Although scientists disagree over the evidence for global warming, since 1992 the need to reduce the levels of carbon-dioxide emissions has been agreed by many countries.

CARBON DIOXIDE OUTPUT

Carbon dioxide forms about one-half of the total amount of greenhouse gases in the air. The pie chart below shows the principal sources of carbon-dioxide emissions. Industrialized countries are now taking action to reduce the output of greenhouse gases into the atmosphere. But the cost of pollution controls is often too high for developing countries.

Residential and commercial [16%]

Deforestation [23%]

Industry [16%]

Electricity [22.5%]

Transportation [22.5%]

Smoke from the furnaces of steel mills fills the air in the Kuzbass industrial region of Siberia, Russia (*right*).

Reflected heat

Sunlight

Greenhouse gases

Trapped heat

HEAT FROM THE SUN

The sun's rays have to pass through the atmosphere to reach the earth. As the rays are reflected back toward space, the layer of greenhouse gases helps to do two things: It absorbs the heat from the sunlight, and it reflects some rays onto the earth's surface.

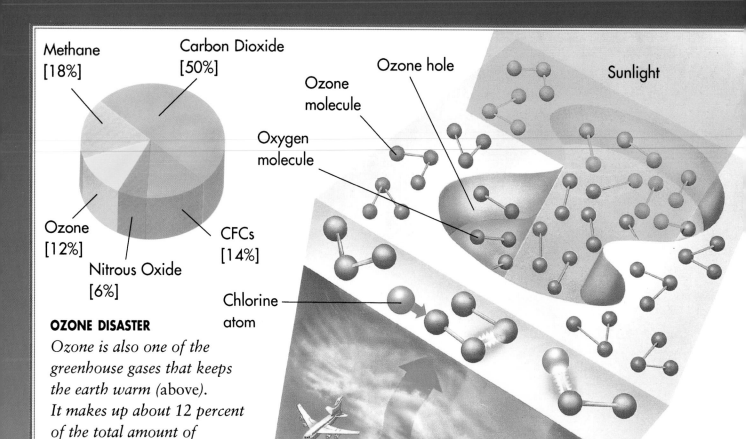

Methane [18%]

Carbon Dioxide [50%]

Ozone [12%]

Nitrous Oxide [6%]

CFCs [14%]

Ozone molecule

Oxygen molecule

Ozone hole

Sunlight

Chlorine atom

OZONE DISASTER

Ozone is also one of the greenhouse gases that keeps the earth warm (above). It makes up about 12 percent of the total amount of greenhouse gases.
The "hole" in the ozone layer is caused mainly by chlorine atoms in chlorofluorocarbons (CFCs) in the atmosphere (right). One atom of chlorine can break up as many as 100,000 molecules of ozone.

CFCs released into atmosphere

1 Sunlight breaks down CFCs and releases atoms of chlorine.

2 The released chlorine atoms attack ozone molecules, pulling away atoms of oxygen from ozone to form chlorine monoxide.

3 Chlorine monoxide combines with another oxygen atom and releases more chlorine atoms, ensuring that the ozone destruction continues.

DANGER IN THE SUN

Sunbathers need to take extra care when exposing their skin to ultraviolet-B rays (left). These harmful rays cause severe sunburn and can lead to skin cancer. Other risks to humans include difficulties in fighting infections and an increased likelihood of eye disorders such as cataracts.

The ozone hole

"Everybody should be alarmed about this. It's far worse that we thought." Michael Kurylo, NASA, 1992

About 12 to 15 miles (20 to 25 kilometers) above the earth's surface there is a layer of invisible ozone gas, a form of oxygen. Down on the ground, ozone occurs in smog (*see* page 20), and is harmful to our eyes and lungs. But high up in the earth's atmosphere, it stops harmful ultraviolet-B rays in sunlight from reaching us.

Scientists believe that this fragile ozone layer is being damaged by certain chemicals, particularly chlorofluorocarbons (CFCs) and halons. We use CFCs as cleaning agents, as a coolant in refrigerators and air-conditioning units, and to manufacture some kinds of plastic foam. Halons are used in fire extinguishers. When released into the atmosphere, they give off chlorine, which attacks and breaks down the ozone layer. Some CFCs have remained unchanged in the atmosphere for more than 100 years.

Scientists reacted with horror when a "hole" was detected in the protective ozone layer above Antarctica in 1985. It was clearly visible on satellite images (*above*). The hole was about the same size as the entire United States, and was equal in depth to the height of Mount Everest.

Scientists from the British Antarctic Survey constantly monitor the ozone levels in Antarctica (*above*).

SPY IN THE SKY

High above the earth, orbiting satellites (left), as well as specially adapted spyplanes, continue to monitor the levels of ozone in the atmosphere. They also send back data concerning the levels of CFCs and other dangerous industrial chemicals that are being released into the atmosphere.

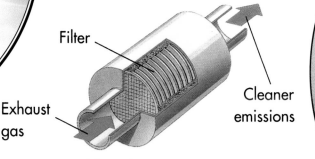

THE BATTLE AGAINST SMOG

Catalytic converters (below) can be installed in the exhaust system of some cars to break down the toxic by-products in exhaust fumes (left) into less harmful substances. There are a number of disadvantages to these devices, however. Catalytic converters themselves produce two greenhouse gases: carbon dioxide and nitrous oxide.

Filter

Exhaust gas

Cleaner emissions

Smog and acid rain

"Acid rain spares nothing. What has taken millennia to evolve is being destroyed in a matter of years." *Don Hinrichson in* The Earth Report, *1988*

Cities such as Los Angeles, Mexico City in Mexico, and Athens in Greece are choked with foul-smelling smog. Cyclists and traffic police have to wear face masks (*right*) to reduce the harmful effects of this filthy air. Smog irritates people's eyes, nose, and lungs; it causes headaches and sickness, and it makes breathing difficult. Long-term damage includes respiratory illnesses, such as asthma and bronchitis, and cancer.

This poisonous soup that fills our cities is called photochemical smog. The harmful gases in car exhaust fumes, which include hydrocarbons, nitrogen dioxide, and carbon monoxide, react together in the air to form the dangerous substances, such as ground-level ozone and

sulfuric acid, that make up smog. Measures to reduce smog levels include reductions in vehicle emissions and the banning of cars altogether in city centers.

Another effect of air pollution is acid rain. Although rain is naturally acidic, it can be increasingly acidified by polluting gases. When these gases dissolve in water droplets, they form acids that fall back to the ground as acid rain or snow. Acid rain damages or kills trees, poisons fish in lakes, and causes long-term damage to soil and water.

Photochemical smog is produced by the action of sunlight on the gases given off in car exhaust fumes (*right*).

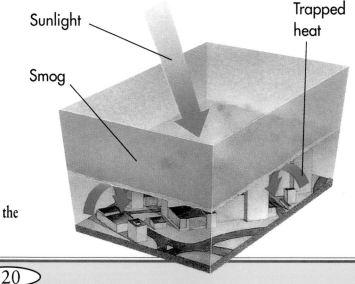

Sunlight

Trapped heat

Smog

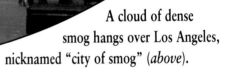

A cloud of dense
smog hangs over Los Angeles,
nicknamed "city of smog" (*above*).

ACID RAIN

Acid rain destroys forests and arable lands, corrodes metal, attacks concrete, and eats away at stonework. The photograph (left) shows a cast of a sculpture made in 1851. The photograph (right) shows the same sculpture today, after it has been exposed to acid rain. Acid rain is causing damage to many of the world's historic monuments, such as the Sphinx in Egypt.

Radiation alert

"There's no future here...no food to buy, and it's not safe to eat anything you grow." *Resident, Narodychi (near Chernobyl), Ukraine*

Radiation is all around us. It is a form of energy given off naturally by the sun and other objects in space, and from rocks and minerals in the earth. Artificially produced radiation is used in science and industry. Mostly, the levels of radiation in the air do not affect us, but larger doses can cause illness and even death.

Nuclear power plants produce high levels of radiation, which is contained within walls of thick concrete and steel. Despite strict safety regulations, accidents occasionally happen at nuclear power stations. If radiation leaks out, it can spread over a wide area, carried by the wind.

On April 26, 1986, the world's worst nuclear accident occurred at the Chernobyl power plant in Ukraine.

One of the four nuclear reactors exploded, releasing clouds of deadly radioactive gas that contaminated thousands of square miles of land. As many as 4.9 million people living in the Ukraine, Belarus, and Russia have been affected by the tragic accident. Within ten days of the disaster, a radioactive cloud had spread beyond Europe, even reaching the United States.

Following the accident, over 150,000 people from nearby villages were forced to leave their homes. The large army of helpers who moved in to clean up the surrounding area received extremely high doses of radiation and are now at the risk of contracting cancer.

Scientists in protective suits use Geiger counters (*right*) to monitor the radiation levels around Chernobyl.

A NEAR MISS

In 1979, the reactor of the Three Mile Island nuclear power plant in Pennsylvania overheated, threatening to release radioactive material into the surrounding area. The plant's technicians managed to prevent the disaster. Ten years after the accident, protesters (left) were still concerned about the safety of the nuclear plant.

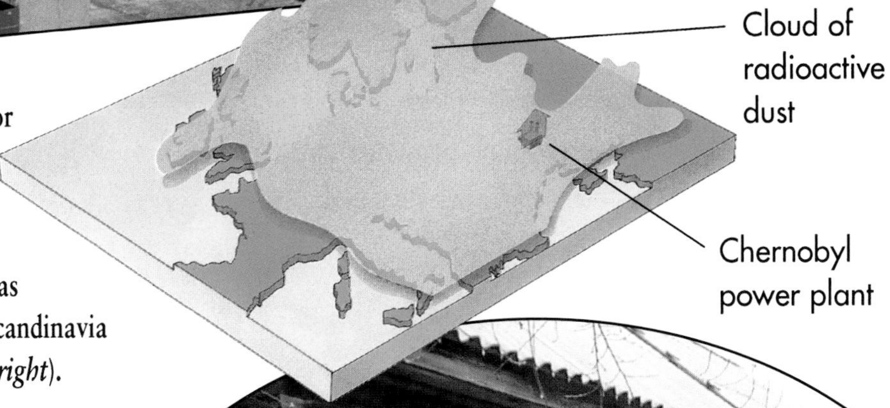

After the accident, the damaged reactor at Chernobyl (*above*) was covered with a giant "coffin" of steel and concrete. Within two days of the disaster, a cloud of radioactive dust was carried by winds across Poland into Scandinavia and over much of the rest of Europe (*right*).

Cloud of radioactive dust

Chernobyl power plant

NO-GO AREA

*After the accident, every town and village within a 40-mile (65-km) radius of Chernobyl was cleared of all its residents (*right*). A few elderly locals returned to some of the 75 deserted villages in the "no-go" evacuated area. Deciding that the risks of radiation are less important than living in their own homes, these people are now growing food and raising livestock on the contaminated land.*

VOLCANIC CLOUDS

Following a massive eruption of Mount Pinatubo in the Philippines in 1991 (left), huge columns of dust and ash billowed upward into the air. Some finally reached as high as 25 miles (40 km) above the ground. The ash clouds were so dense that they blotted out the sunlight, turning day into night. Thousands of tribespeople in the area had to be evacuated from their villages.

Clouds of gas

"The air seemed to be normal, yet all around me people were choking." *Survivor, Bhopal, India, 1984*

Gas leaks from chemical factories can be extremely dangerous. Winds carry poisonous gases across a wide area, affecting anyone who comes into contact with them. Disaster struck the central Indian city of Bhopal on December 2, 1984. Clouds of highly poisonous gas leaked from the American-owned Union Carbide pesticide factory. More than 2,000 people died instantly. Hundreds of thousands of others living nearby were severely affected by the gas (*see* page 25).

Escapes of poisonous gas can also be due to natural causes. In 1986, in the West African country of Cameroon, a deadly jet of carbon dioxide gas escaped from Lake Nios

one night. The gas drifted toward the village of Lower Nios in the valley below. A total of 1,700 villagers died in Lower Nios and surrounding villages. When local herdsmen returned the next day, they found the bodies of people and animals all over the village. The cloud of gas had even destroyed the flies and vultures that would have usually swooped down to attack dead cattle.

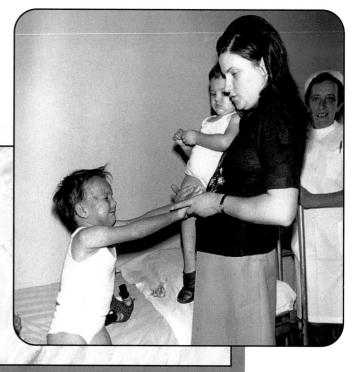

CHILDREN AT RISK

A dangerous poison called dioxin leaked from a herbicide plant in the Italian town of Seveso in 1976. Following the accident, Europe's worst-ever case of industrial pollution, the town had to be evacuated. Several years after the accident, many children were still suffering from rashes and burns, and other skin complaints (right).

DEADLY CLOUDS

An entire shantytown had grown up around the Union Carbide factory walls, housing thousands of Bhopal's poorest residents. The poisonous gas blew through their flimsy homes in an instant, killing or blinding some people immediately (below). As the clouds of poisonous gas filled the air over the city, many people in the immediate area of the pesticide factory experienced breathing problems (left). Many more died later as a result of contamination by the deadly gas, and more than 200,000 people suffered injuries.

INSECTS ON THE MOVE

A locust (below) is any kind of short-horned grasshopper. Some of these grasshoppers are migratory, usually after the females have laid their eggs. During a single breeding season, a female locust can lay hundreds of eggs. When their breeding grounds become crowded, the young locusts grow restless and start to migrate in swarms to other areas (right).

RED-BILLED PESTS

The tiny red-billed quelea bird (left) lives in Africa, feeding mainly on seeds. When searching for food, queleas collect in huge flocks numbering millions of birds. The size of the flocks has led some countries to label these birds as pests because of the damage that such large flocks can inflict on crops and other vegetation.

Pests in the air

"The swarm of locusts was so dense, they turned the sky black as night." *Villager, North Africa, 1995*

Some birds and insects fly together in large groups, called flocks or swarms. They do this for a variety of reasons. Wasps and bees swarm when they are looking for a new nesting place. Blackbirds flock when they are feeding and roosting in the fall and winter — often greatly damaging grain and fruit crops. Another airborne pest is the mosquito. Some carry the germs that cause diseases like malaria and yellow fever. When a mosquito "bites" a human (only the females do this), it may pass these germs into the person's blood.

One of the most destructive swarming insects is the locust. A single swarm might contain up to 50 million individual insects. Plagues of these hungry insects are common when rains fall after a prolonged period of drought, filling the air until there is barely a patch of sky to be seen.

In Africa and the Middle East, they can destroy vast areas of precious crops.

Locusts can eat more than their own body weight of food in just one day. They devour almost any kind of green plant, although grass is their preferred meal. A swarm can strip a whole field of crops in one hour. Attempts to control the movement of locusts include spraying insecticides on the young insects before they are capable of flight, and plowing land in which they have laid their eggs.

MOSQUITO CONTROL

Methods of controlling mosquitoes (above) include spraying buildings, fields, and forest areas with chemicals to kill the insects (right). Another method is to spray or destroy the places where they breed, such as marshes, swamps, ponds, ditches, and pools of stagnant water.

Amazing air

"The clouds formed such fantastic shapes as to look startlingly unnatural" *Sailor witnessing the eruption of Krakatau, 1883*

Air has a mysterious quality because it is invisible. Yet in the natural world around us, we can see some surprising phenomena produced by air on the move. It is responsible for creating some of the most dramatic rock formations found on Earth. Over thousands and sometimes millions of years, the wind has sculpted rocks into some fantastic shapes. It erodes (wears away) the softer parts to form smooth shapes such as the unusual red sandstone ones in Monument Valley in southeastern Utah (*above*). Another wind-shaped formation in Monument Valley, known as the "totem pole," is so tall that it creates a 35-mile (56-kilometer) long shadow in the evening light.

People say that wind can also affect human behavior. When certain winds blow, they are reported to change people's moods. For example, the cold mistral that blows down over France and out across the Mediterranean is said to make people feel irritable. The warm, dry sirocco wind that blows off the Sahara and the hot, dry chinooks in the Rockies are said to have the same effect.

The quality of our air needs to be taken seriously, too. All our scientific knowledge and instruments must be used not only to protect ourselves from hurricanes and tornadoes, but to make sure that future generations can breathe clean air.

"Red sky at night, sailors' delight" — this old weather rhyme means that it will be a fine day after a red sunset.

A MIGHTY BLAST

When the volcanic island of Krakatau in Indonesia exploded in 1883 (right), the blast was so loud that it could be heard in Australia! Dust was blown through the air to places thousands of miles away. The force of the eruption created a huge wave that destroyed villages on nearby islands.

MYSTERIOUS LIGHTS

Colored lights sometimes appear in the night sky in northern and southern parts of the world. This colorful display is known as the "northern (or southern) lights." These lights are given off when tiny particles from the sun reach the earth's atmosphere hundreds of miles above the ground.

A PAIR OF TWISTERS

Tornadoes, or twisters, sometimes arrive in pairs, called "sisters" (right). Sometimes, tornadoes can appear in even bigger groups. In April 1974, a massive outbreak of 148 separate tornadoes struck the United States, appearing over 13 different states during one 24-hour period. A total of 315 people were killed.

Emergency first aid

Here is some practical advice for emergencies involving someone who is having difficulty in breathing:

• Gently lay the person flat on their back, tilt their head backward, and push their chin and jaw upward. This keeps the airway open, so that air can pass into his or her lungs without obstruction.

• If they are unconscious, lie the casualty on their front with their head turned to one side (recovery position).

• If a casualty stops breathing, artificial ventilation is needed to get air back into the person's lungs. This should be carried out only by someone who has been properly trained in the technique.

• IMPORTANT: Remember that first aid is a skilled treatment that could save a person's life. However, if you are not sure how to give first aid, you should quickly find someone nearby who does know.

• Try to help the casualty as best as you can and quickly get them to a doctor or the hospital.

Here are some common causes of breathing difficulties:

• Inhaling car exhaust fumes or smoke from a fire.

• Some people suffer from severe allergic reactions, for example, when they are stung by an insect.

• When a piece of food passes into a person's windpipe instead of the food passage. The blockage can usually be removed by coughing or slapping the back.

• Asthma occurs when the airway narrows and becomes inflamed. Asthma sufferers usually carry an inhaler, which gives a dose of medicine to make breathing easier.

Glossary

Acid rain Rain containing harmful acids that can poison rivers and lakes, kill trees, and damage stonework.

Atmosphere The layers of air that surround the earth.

Catalytic converter A device fitted to a car's exhaust system, which removes harmful substances from the exhaust fumes.

Chlorofluorocarbon (CFC) One of a group of chemicals used in refrigerators and aerosols, and to make foam products.

Cyclone A storm in which very strong winds spiral toward the center.

Desertification The gradual process that changes grassland into a desert area.

Dust devil A whirling column of air.

El Niño A current of warm water that heats up cold water in the Pacific Ocean. It can affect weather patterns all over the world.

Erosion The process of wearing away. The erosion of rocks is carried out by wind and water.

Fossil fuel A fuel, such as coal, oil, and gas, that formed deposits over millions of years from the remains of living things.

Global warming A gradual increase in the temperature of the world.

Greenhouse effect The trapping of the sun's heat by gases in the atmosphere. This heat helps to warm the earth.

Greenhouse gas One of the gases in the atmosphere that traps heat from the sun and prevents it from escaping into space.

Hurricane A powerful storm that brings strong winds and heavy rains. Hurricanes form in tropical areas over the North Atlantic and North Pacific oceans.

Insecticide A chemical sprayed on crops and other plants to kill harmful insects.

Nuclear reactor The main part of a nuclear power plant. It uses nuclear fuel to produce huge amounts of energy, mainly as heat.

Ozone A gas that is found high up in the atmosphere as well as in polluted air on the ground. It is a form of oxygen.

Pesticide A chemical that destroys harmful pests living on plants and animals.

Photochemical smog Polluted air that lies close to the ground. It is caused by the reaction between sunlight and harmful substances in the air.

Pollutant Any substance, particularly waste material, that damages our environment.

Radiation Energy that is given off by something, for example, light rays from the sun. Large doses of radiation can be harmful to living things.

Smog A type of air pollution that forms when smoke and fog mix together.

Storm surge A huge mound of seawater that is whipped up by powerful winds.

Tornado A funnel of swirling winds that stretches from a cloud down to the ground.

Typhoon A hurricanelike storm that forms over the western Pacific Ocean.

Waterspout A tornado that forms over water.

Index

Picture Credits

(t-top, m-middle, b-bottom, r-right, l-left)
All pictures supplied by Frank Spooner Pictures apart from the following: front cover - Rex Features. 13t, 18, 19b & 31 - Pictor International. 13m - Warner Bros/ Universal/ Amblin (courtesy Kobal). 15 - Hulton Getty. 21b both & 28 both - Roger Vlitos. 32t - AEA Technology/ Solution Pictures. 29r - Mary Evans Picture Library.